GEORGE M. NE[

Fashion
Coloring book

FOR GIRLS
AGES 8-12

This book belongs to:

_____

- -

_____

Thank you for purchasing our book.
Our team has worked very hard to
create high quality products.
Every feedback is very important to us
and we read each one very carefully.
It helps us grow, so please
leave reviews on Amazon.

Thank You

Made in the USA
Las Vegas, NV
06 December 2023

82198532R00070